The New Futurist

Olivia Thomas

Published by Olivia Thomas, 2024.

While every precaution has been taken in the preparation of this book, the publisher assumes no responsibility for errors or omissions, or for damages resulting from the use of the information contained herein.

THE NEW FUTURIST

First edition. April 20, 2024.

ISBN: 979-8224735112

Written by Olivia Thomas.

Table of Contents

For the future...

KAIROS I

A specter is haunting America:
The specter of progress.

The elites of our nation,
Have entered into an alliance
To halt this movement,

And breed discord among
The people:
Black and white,
Man and woman,
Gay and straight,
Old and young,
Cis and trans—

Who reading this poem
Has not been called a progressive?
When did such a great aspiration
Become an insult?

It is time that we talk about

What happened to cause this war...

The Starfish Poem

While walking along the beach,
I spotted a young girl
Throwing starfish into the ocean.
I inquired into her quest,
To which she replied, "All these starfish are going to die!
Someone's got to save them!"
"But you can't save all these starfish," I told her,
"Most of them are bound to die anyway."
"It doesn't matter how many I save,
Only that I save as many as I can."
Not being able to refute her,
I joined her,
And soon many others joined too.

But what are starfish?
What is the ocean?
Why do so many creatures die in such a manner?
Is it their destiny to die
Upon the dry, forgotten shore?
Is it our duty to save them,
Even if it is God's decision
To have them killed?
Does He will it,
Or does humanity will it?
Is this the result of some tidal shift
Or algal bloom?

We did not worry,
Only continuing our battle
Against the mighty ocean.

God may not give us much,
But at least he gives us starfish to throw.

My First Memory

I remember sitting on my kitchen floor
With a child's watercolor set
And a sheet of printer paper,
Painting pictures of rainbows
Before my mother got home.

I think it was that night she told me
About how two planes flew into the Twin Towers.
We didn't know who did it then
Or why
Only that they were evil
And there was evil in the world.

Recipe for a New Body

Ingredients

- 1 FitBit™ monitor
- 1 gym membership
- 1 fitness coach
- 1 carton of Halo Top™ Ice Cream
- 1 Mexican tapeworm (contained inside a capsule)
- 1 plastic surgeon
- 1 skincare routine
- 1 pair of almond shaped eyes (preferably blue)
- 1 8-ball
- 6-12 inches of hair (preferably blonde)
- 50 units of Botox
- Bronzer
- Infinite money

Instructions

1. Prepare a large cauldron and fill it with water. Immerse your entire body in it and allow your plastic surgeon to help you out of it when they feel as if all your imperfections have been washed away.

2. Have your plastic surgeon place you into an ultraviolet coffin. The coffin will absorb any remaining water and cause your skin to burn, which is a sign that you should immediately apply bronzer.
3. During this process, your plastic surgeon will begin injecting you with botox. At this point, you should feel your hair being bleached and your eyes turning a pure, radiant blue.
4. After that is over, you should immediately apply your skincare routine, and continue to do so once every day for the rest of your life. You should also swallow the capsule containing the tapeworm. If you happen to consume Ben & Jerry's rather than Halo Top, the tapeworm will correct this.
5. Your fitness coach will attach the FitBit™ monitor to you in order to make sure you stay healthy, which will launch your career as a supermodel. He will also give you your gym membership, your 8-ball, and (if you wish) roughly one million followers on Instagram.

American Roulette

Go on
Take a shot:
They start at only a couple of dollars.
If you want, buy some more;
Your chances will double
Triple
Quadruple
Quintuple.

Watch how that ball spins!
Up, down, up, down,
Buy low! Sell high!
You can make a guess,
But there's no guarantee:
It's all up to the hand
You can't see.

If you win,
It's the American Dream,
But if you lose,
Well, that's just business, baby.

Airports

How like the Americans!
So many opportunities for travel!

Forward right, backward left,
Transition from terminal to terminal.

Arrive at least two hours early!
You don't want to miss your chance!

How much for a checked bag?
Will my carry-on fit?

Don't talk to me on the plane!
I have headphones and a book!

Where should I stop for lunch?
Or is it time for breakfast?

So many shops line the streets!
So many places to spend money!

Would it have been cheaper to drive?
Should I have taken the train?

I love flying and I love transportation!

Elon Musk

Elon Musk says that there is no one he wants to help more
Than Gen Z,
So much that he is willing to take us all the way to Mars
To end poverty.

He says—
But what a billionaire says to everyday people
Is fitting to be written
On wind and rushing water.

My Worst Uber Driver

It was on one of those occasions
That I had to go to the hospital,
And I couldn't afford an ambulance,
So I took an Uber.

The driver never asked why I was going
(And, for that matter, I don't even remember why),
But he sure had a lot to say about himself:

He had wanted to be an airline pilot,
Even going to school for it.
The tuition was expensive,
The training was difficult.
As competitive as it was,
It's no wonder he didn't make it,
And ended up as an Uber driver.

I think about that ride now and then,
Living in my small, roach-infested apartment,
Waiting for my EBT card to arrive,
And wishing I was a writer.

I Am the City

I am the city
Who never sleeps at night
That doesn't open the bars at five
And always brings the streets to life.

And I walk through the city.

I am the city
Where there are many things to do
That many people pass through
And always has a nice view.

And I ride through the city.

I am the city
Where many people live
That always has something to give
Which almost makes a bridge.

And I don't drive to the city,
But I fly to the city.

Where are You From?

Where am I from?
Oh, you've probably never heard of it.
It's a really small town
About halfway between Asheville and Charlotte.

It's called Boiling Springs;
Right outside of Shelby.
Have you heard of Shelby?
Well, it's the city closest to it,
Though some say it isn't even a real city.
And I suppose it isn't.

I usually just tell people I'm from North Carolina.
Just, "a small town in North Carolina."
Nowhere special, nowhere interesting.
Nowhere connected to the rest of the world.

Modern Poems Require Modern Illusions

When my old Latin teacher Bessie heard I planned to major in classics in college,
She told me, "Leave it to one of the Henkel boys to want to study Latin,
Only a real scholar would want to do that."
But because I couldn't take my eyes off my phone for ten minutes,
I simply rolled my eyes and said, "Okay boomer."

Indeed, many of my classmates thought the same thing,
Saying things like, "Much smart. Very intelligence. Wow."
When it came to the Latin language,
I was the only one around who could firmly grasp it.
They all ran from it as if it was a stuffed rat in a grocery store.
I wasn't like other girls.

Nevertheless, I understood their distaste for it.
A dead language?
Ain't nobody got time for that!
But I understood Bessie in her reasoning behind teaching,
"They *really* need some education up at Burns High School!"
It wasn't much, but it was honest work.

I entered college eventually,
Which I was looking forward to.

It felt like I had been waiting for eighty-four years.
I thought I was prepared,
But it came like an egregiously loud moan.
I was like SpongeGar,
Though my brain was only growing smaller and smaller.
I was shooketh.

I learned many things in order to fit into my new environment.
I forgot that Bush did 9/11,
And learned how to construct Latin and Greek declension tables.
My best friends became poems,
And my lovers became Catullus, Ovid, and Sulpicia.
"Dicks Out for Harambe" no longer sounded poetic to me.
Instead, I was much more content with the rhythm of iambic pentameter.

I forgot that Jeffrey Epstein didn't kill himself,
And learned to avoid using passive voice in an essay,
Though a professor would later teach me this was prescriptive.
I still never learned the etymology of Arkansas.

I think a part of me will still prefer "whomst" over "whom,"
Despite my red shirt being exchanged for a full tuxedo.
I've always wanted to be as brave as Linda Glocke someday,
Or at least brave enough to yell, "I'm a bad bitch! You can't kill me!"

But someone had to hold me back from yelling at the cat.
It was time for me to release my clenched fist.

So I dyed and tied up my hair,
Reduced my breasts,
And enlightened my skin—
All because I picked up a book.

After all, we *do* live in a society.
Really makes you think, doesn't it?

English Has No Future

"The English language has no future," they'd say,
Before invading foreign lands
To establish churches in the Global South,
And rip out the tongues of barbarian peoples.

Aliens would descend from the heavens
Armored with the two most dangerous weapons:
Guns and books,
Including the most dangerous book of all:
τὸ βιβλίον,
A book that could hang witches and shed blood,
But only if it is written in the extraterrestrial language.

Hitler too had this mentality.
Why shouldn't German be the language of Germany?
It definitely shouldn't be Yiddish;
You can see Hebrew in their noses and hair.

ero erimus
eris eritis
erit erunt

I never thought of flowers when thinking of Ancient Rome,
Only dust and ruined temples.
I only remembered the gladiators' bloodshed in the arena,
The fire and salt upon the soil of Carthage,

And how Nero played the violin as the city of Rome burned
to the ground.

If only Virgil had succeeded in destroying the Aeneid.

Bar bar, said the foreigners,
Bar bar.

Some may say Latin is dead,
But it lives on in Italian, Spanish, French...
How can something so dead live so long?
How can one nation have so much power even after it has
fallen?
After all, West is Best.

If Ancient Rome and Ancient Greece were its building
blocks,
Then the entire Western World would surely fall.
Pay no mind that it already did.
Or that it is made up of heathens and heretics.

    I shall be   *We shall be*
    You will be   *You all will be*
He/she/it will be *They will be*

A woman emerges from the subway:
She is lonely in a crowd of people she does not recognize,
Lost—and afraid.

She sees another woman just like her,
And immediately she feels at home.
¿Dónde está el restaurante más cercano? she asks.
Está en la primera calle a la derecha, she responds.
Gracias. And means it.

But then a large man with a red hat approaches them to yell,
"This is America! Speak English!"

They stop their conversation out of fear.

> *Mi estos* *Ni estos*
> *Ci estos* *Vi estos*
> *Li/ŝi/ĝi estos Ili estos*

The worlds will be destroyed,
And in their place, only one—
The true one.

A lingua franca will be established,
And with it a *cultura franca,*
A Pax Romana.

Neither singing nor games,
Only the long-forgotten notion of true equality,
And the spirit of many with the mind of one.

Teaching Icarus How to Fly

Boy, you better flap those wings:
The eagles are chasing after you.
They'll tear out your liver,
And jump through hurdles,
Though the sky is falling above you.

How stupid can you be?
Wax melts under the heat.
Wear your honored toga
While you conquer the sun!

Take up your victory:
The war with nature is done.
The consequence of government action
Will go on to show your worth.

Be wary of the products you've produced,
Even though they are yours to keep.
As long as the sunlight keeps its power,
The science will continue to climb.

Breaking the Glass Ceiling

I can see them now
Beneath us.
Beneath the glass.

Like airplanes
They fly up
And up
Until their engines stall
And they can do nothing
But fall down.

These monsters must be desperate
And hungry
If they think they can break
Unbreakable glass.

And I can feel them seeping in
They want what's ours,
What we've so desperately protected.

They want it for themselves,
But they already have so much.

If they break it,
Everything falls apart
Then falls back into place.

Violence in America

I wake up, get out of bed,
Take a shower, make some coffee,
An innocent black man is shot by police,
Eat some breakfast, brush my teeth,
Get in my car, and go to work.

I get out of my car, walk into the building,
Sit down at my desk, open up my computer,
Twenty children are killed in a school shooting,
Get some coffee, talk to my coworkers,
Check my email, and plan for the day.

I exit the building, drive home,
Walk into my apartment, change clothes,
Almost a million are sent to die in a foreign country,
Cook dinner, watch some TV,
Read a book, and fall asleep.

The Fermi Paradox

I stole a rocket from Area 51
In order to sail off into space
And see those aliens.

I explored the galaxy,
Making my way out to Venus,
Hoping to find what remained
Of a civilization destroyed by climate change.
Only to find a human-like species,
Though its origin was inconclusive.

I made my way out to Mars,
Landing on its red and rocky surface,
Not Communist but bloody and traditional.
I only ever saw Elon Musk and his crew,
Preparing to build for us a new planet,
That would one day itself be called "alien."

I thought that the planet being red would make it a warm planet,
But it is not.
It is cold,
And dark,
And empty.

And it does not have much gravity.
The gravitational pull is so small
That one would not survive more than one Martian year.

Why do we want to establish a colony here?
Though it is in the Goldilocks zone,
Perhaps there is a planet that is more just-right
Somewhere beyond.

I even journeyed out to Jupiter's Europa,
Breaking the ice and its cold murky surface.
It was as if they were still waiting
For their Cambrian explosion,
Deep within an invisible sea,

But I quickly lost hope.
Though it was vastly different from Mars,
It was still cold, dark, and empty.
Even though water is necessary for life,
Too much, and you will drown.

Unsatisfied,
I ventured out into the stars,
Each and every one of them.
I carved a tally mark into my skin for every
Galaxy cluster,
Stellar cluster,
Solar system
That did not contain it
Until my body was an artificial fossil,
A foggy memory of what possibly could've existed.

24

I prayed to God for wisdom,
Sent out radio signals,
Learned every language that could ever exist,
Even broke the dimensions of time and space
In order to look
Beyond the conceivable universe...
I hacked into the matrix,
Mastered Sims 5,
Only to find that every time I

    Blew out my brains,
    Threw a toaster into the bathtub,
    Tied a noose around my neck,
    Swallowed a countless amount of antidepressants—
    Still woke up on that infamous Groundhog Day.

The orbit and tidal lock were too powerful
For the Universe's gravitas.
It doesn't exist here or there.

And so I waited,
And waited,
For them to find me.
Yet they were right in front of my face,
A facetious poltergeist,
Laughing in some incomprehensible language,
At such a pathetic creature
That would dare to colonize the stars.

So now I head home

To an alien planet
Only to find that the doomsday clock
Has already struck midnight.

Celestial

Stephen Hawking was not supposed to live past twenty-three,
But he did.
After he died, his ashes were launched into space,
Creating tiny meteor showers to rain upon the Earth.

Sometimes I wonder if he's in some other dimension,
And the gamma radiation he is creating,
Is his wisdom to receive for all mankind.

But he is more than just his wisdom.
He is an idea,
A philosophy of our potentiality
Against the wind of resistance,
An elegy of the Anthropocene Extinction.

The Battle of the Binary Star System

We have been together since birth,
Having arisen from the molecular cloud.
Two stars, yet one solar system,
And that is how we were known to many.

For millennia I orbited you,
And together we nurtured the life of our orbiting children:
The expansiveness was ours to share.

But you were stronger than I was,
And bigger,
And I became jealous.

And so I said,
"Give it to me!
For millions of years I have orbited you,
And you have given me nothing in return.
Now I wish to occupy the barycenter."

And without your consent, I took it,
Your hydrogen, helium,
Elements that had taken you centuries to build.
I spun around like an ice dancer,
A tornado of fury.
You became a part of me,
And I was no longer a part of you.

I was growing brighter,
And in return,
You could only grow dimmer.

But I could not keep my secrets:
From me you learned,
Like a child learns from a parent,
The cycle of violence.

And without my consent, you took it,
My carbon, oxygen,
Elements that had taken me years to build.
You spun around like an ice dancer,
A tornado of fury.
I became a part of you,
But you were no longer a part of me.

The universe begged that we end our fighting,
Yet demanded that one of us must come out victorious.

And now you learn to lose control,
Strip away your layers,
And bring about an iron age:
A split-second of ethereal energy.

But you will create destruction,
And beauty for those light-years away.

The Stars in North Carolina

I didn't get to see the stars
Often in Tulsa
Because of light pollution.

Even though I love the Big City,
I missed standing in a field at night
With every possible heaven above me.

It made me feel closer
To whatever could be up there.

Perhaps one day
I can reach out
And something else
Can reach in
And we can form our own
Metropolis.

A Poem about the Rain

I was supposed to write a poem
About the rain,
And how it reminded me of

Sadness,
A sad day,
Depression,
Darkness and gloominess,
Blood from the war,
Destruction,
God washing away our sins,
A baptism,
A shower,
A bath,
A flood,
Thunder,
Lightning,
And the pain of existence,

But when I sat down to write it,

Warm mugs of coffee or tea,
Cats and dogs sleeping on a couch,
Reading a book on a Saturday afternoon,
Napping on a bed with the curtains open,
Splashing in puddles,
The tingles I get from ASMR,

Hugging someone underneath an umbrella,
Being wrapped in a warm blanket,
The city,
And gently falling asleep

Were all I could think of.

Phoenix

You burned me once,
And I hated you for that;
Everyone's burned me at some point,
Because fire is life.

Phlogiston escaping,
My muscles start to break.
I internally exhale
A black cloud of relief.

My bed becomes a temple,
An altar for sacrifice.
Entrails unfold gold
That I must collect.

A sun shines through my window:
It is my mother saying
That I *must* go home
With empty open wings.

Reflecting Light

Often glass can seem more like a mirror.
When one looks,
They expect to see the other side
But instead see a collage of windows
Reflecting each other's light.

I was a piece of glass once,
Hidden inside a dark closet.
The light from under the door was faint,
But it was there.
With this light I saw wood,
And from wood created fire.
From this, I created more fire,
Which created more light.

Together we found other glass people
And we stretched our light
To the darkest parts of the universe.
Our union created places of worship
And greenhouses growing dunes of sand.

KAIROS II

There have always been two classes of people:
The owners and the owned.

In ancient Rome,
There were patricians and plebeians,
Where the plebeians were a parasite
Upon the patricians.

In modern America,
There were masters and slaves,
Where the masters were a parasite
Upon the slaves.

Society has always existed within binaries.
With one being heavier than the other.
But what if they were equal?
What if they never existed at all?

These ends are like binary stars:
One stands at one end
Slowly devouring the other.

Many people blame the cities,
But this happens in the country too.
Violence exists everywhere.

36

One day this may end,
But the universe is shameless,
And will stop at nothing,
To keep itself in power.

It doesn't trickle down.
It never trickles down.

I admit the sun has done a lot:
Created life,
Evolved it,
Given it a home,
Centralized.

We owe it a lot,
Don't we?
We owe the owners nothing.

We depend on each other,
Yet we are destroying each other.

Once the stars were separate,
Doing their own thing,
But once one saw the power of the other
And desired to take some for itself,
Something new was created
From the ashes.

Everything that was property

Would then become art.

If we are to continue in this endeavor,
Then every star must be destroyed.

Not Another Love Song

I'm fucking sick of love songs,
And I'm fucking sick of writing them.

But what other release do I have?

I gave up cutting myself,
Hookups and dating apps,
Even masturbation and pornography,

But why does the blood still run
Like shots of vodka
Through my veins?

I thought the antidote would make it stop;
That becoming a woman would make me less of a man,

But I am still a hunter,
An animal ready to devour
And be devoured.

An Abundance of John Does

John #0

I only remember your face,
Or rather, your profile picture.
I didn't see your face that often.

Actually, I don't remember that much about you.
I think you were the one with the trans boyfriend.
I envy him for discovering himself so soon.

I think of all that people in the group chat,
You were the one I knew the least.
I talked to so many others,
And got to know all their little quirks.
Their little personality traits.
But all I remember about you is your shaggy hair,
And that drawn profile picture.

I had a crush on everyone in that group chat.
It's how I was trained to act,
Not by you,
But by the men who found me before.

Did you meet them too?
We all came from that same website.
I was so proud of my page there.
I thought my memes were so funny.

Apparently the guys who dmed me thought so too.
At least, that's what they'd tell me.

Putting my Kik in my bio didn't seem like a bad idea at the time.
I liked the attention.
I don't remember how often it was.
Maybe a few times a month?
I don't think I remember any of them.
I think I tried to forget them actually.

All I remember is the excitement I felt after getting a message,
And being asked my age, sex, and location.
Being told to send a face pic.
Being told I looked really cute.
Being told they were horny.
Being asked if I wanted to see.
Being asked if I was horny too.
Being asked to see.

Everyone always warned me about online predators.
I was told what they looked like,
And they looked nothing like that.

What wasn't to want?
I was a boy.
A teenage boy.
I was supposed to want sex.
How could I say no?

I wasn't supposed to say no.

I really did want it, though.
None of the guys my age—
Or in real life—
Had any interest in me, anyway,
Or even knew I liked them.

These men were my pornotopia.
What others saw as hell,
I saw as Eden.
And God told me to worship him.

John, if you met those men too...
They were just pictures on a screen,
Like you were a picture on my phone.

We were just kids then, weren't we?

John #1

It had only been a month since I tride to commit suicide.

I had downloaded it before,
But immediately deleted it after
Because I was afraid;
I knew the men wouldn't like me—
Or at least the ones my own age.

I didn't expect you to message so soon.

42

People were still getting back from Thanksgiving break,
So there was plenty of time
And space.

And I knew my roommate wouldn't be back until the last
minute.
He would never know my dirty little secret.

You looked different from the picture you sent me,
But I said nothing.
Who was I to reject you?
I didn't say no.
You never say no.

I don't remember how we got our clothes off.
The first thing I do remember is how forcefully you kissed me,
And that it was my first kiss.
We made out for a while,
But I never closed my eyes.
Yours terrified me.

I eventually asked you to fuck me in the ass.
And you did.
I didn't ever wonder
Whether I was a top or a bottom.
I was just used to getting fucked.

All the while, you kept staring at me
With those goddamn eyes.

I could've sworn you wanted to kill me.

I couldn't wait for it to be over,
But I didn't say no.
I never said no.
You don't say no.

It was certainly not rape
In the traditional sense.
I was supposed to lie back and take it,
Empty and motionless.

Before it was over, I thought,
Was I really gay?
I didn't enjoy it
Yet. Would I ever?

I tried to feed it back,
Begging you to say no,
But you were just as desperate
As I was.

I did say no when you met me a second time,
But by then you were already my first.

John #2

You were the only good thing about that trip.
I learned a lot from the workshops,
But the most about myself from you.

44

We met at that speed dating thing.
I was nervous about finding someone;
I wasn't expecting to meet anyone.

But then we were at the same table.

I don't remember much between us.
But I remember that you gave your number
To me.

I didn't know what to think.
How could someone so beautiful
Want someone like me?

You didn't know anything about the men I fucked for fun.
If you knew about that,
Then maybe you would've thought
I just wanted to fuck you.
I think you did
And you didn't care.

You wanted to get to know,
When I just wanted to know your body,
Or so I thought.
I found that surprising,
Since I was used to men just wanting my body,
Not who I was as a person.

Was I really supposed to?
Was I really allowed to?

If we had more time,
Maybe I could've,
And to be honest,
I probably should've.
It's all I would've done now.

We didn't have much time.
We spent it just the two of us,
With no one else around.

I was so stupid to suggest it,
But you didn't say no,
You never said no.

I felt ashamed afterwards.
How could you have treated me so well,
When all I gave you was my body?

Didn't I?

I cried myself to sleep that night.

John #3

We met on Grindr,
Talked for months,
But never met in person.

I'd finally found a boyfriend
When you got back.

I don't have much to say about you,
Other than that you hit me up
When you still had a girlfriend.

There was never gonna be anything serious between us
Other than sex.

Still, we made each other so many promises:
You had a private space
Where we could fuck,
And I said I'd be down whenever.

I'm glad we never met up;
You weren't even that hot.
And you were a Republican.

The person I met after—
The one that saved me from you—
Was so much better.

"You're gonna have a boyfriend
Before we ever get a chance to meet,"
You said, and yeah,
I fucking did.
And he was the best goddamn thing
That ever happened to me.

Our first date was at Pride.
He insisted on paying,
Because it was his idea.
He insisted on paying for everything.

I still remember
When we first held hands,
When he grabbed my arm
And our fingers just sort of
Fell together.

I still remember
When we first kissed,
When he was dropping me off
From our third date
And I asked if he was my boyfriend,
Because I genuinely didn't know.

And I still remember
When we first had sex.
When we talked about just taking a nap,
We both knew we were kidding.

I was so glad I ended up with him
Instead of you,
Because as straight as it might sound,
He made me feel like a real woman.

Be Yourself

Myself is a heart that won't quit pounding,
A set of lungs that can't get air,
And a brain that won't shut up.

Myself is having a panic attack
Right before I meet someone new.

Myself is freaking out
Just because I have a crush on a guy.

Myself is the wave of sadness I feel
After a large social gathering.

Myself is wanting to be female
But having the body of a man.

Myself is going nonverbal
When I trip over my words.

Myself is feeling lonely
In the company of other people.

Myself is thinking I'm annoying
When someone can't hang out with me.

Myself is laying in bed,

And doing nothing.

Myself is sitting in front of a computer
And doing nothing.

Myself is not falling asleep
Or not waking up.

Myself is a car not going
When I step on the gas.

Third Person

What will he think?
What will he say?

She wants to approach him.
She wants to ask him out.

She will tell him all she is thinking,
About her way of life.

He thinks she is mad,
Doesn't he?

She makes no mistake.
She can only move forward.

He pulls out his phone, though,
Still listening to her...blunder?

She relates what she can,
But she wants to kiss him.

He gives a smile:
Will he?

She stays.
He leaves.

One day he may return,
But he will never say.

Language of the Unheard

I always say I'm a socialist when I'm sad,
And a communist when I'm angry.

Most days I'm sad,
But lately I've been angry.
So fucking angry.

Everyday I watch my sisters die,
Not by choice but out of necessity,
As a way of reetching their names
Scrapped off in *damnatio memoriae*.
They say these chisels are guns,
But we have no wish to keep them.

I have visions of Liberation Army Dreamers,
Except these soldiers will not die in vain.
I will lead them straight to the courthouse,
And open vessels of red upon the streets,
Flooding cities and towns with our insides.
Our final form will be a light in the darkness.

Turning the wine back into water—
Then back again—
Leave no stone unturned:
We didn't start the culture war.
No, we've been fighting for our lives,

And self-defense is the perfect excuse.

Parasocial Relationships (Reading Poetry Part 2)

I want to consume you.

I saw you deep in the lake,
A mirror staring back at me.
I'd never seen someone so beautiful.

I wanted to touch you,
And drown in you,
Beautiful soul of a poet.

What a mistake it was:
What a mistake it could've been.

You were not a liar,
Only a storyteller.

I thought life imitated art.
But nothing so lifelike—
So divine—
Could dent the bronze statue.

You have set me on fire,
And you don't even know who I am.

You are a vision on the screen,

Fictional and invisible,
Though not quite digital.
What am I supposed to do with that?
It is priceless and free.
No drop of blood will bring you to life,
Even if only for a moment.

I feel so fucking crazy,
Inside your house,
Smelling your clothes.

I want to strangle you,
So that your death will make me live
Forever.

I don't think that's possible.

The Ending

Our day is done.

The murder's been solved,
The battle's been won.

Let's hold a wedding
For the happy couple.
Happily ever after:
I'm sure they never fight.

May we put them on a Grecian urn.
We can worship them and remember them
Forever.

"All good things must come to an end,"
They say.
But does it really?

What is the answer?
What is the conclusion?

Touch the Flame

Damn Prometheus,
Why did you give us light
In the form of fire?

Fire is pure carnage.
You brought it for warmth,
But all I want is destruction
Of myself,
Of others,
And all of society.

What I seek is electricity,
That moves through my blood
With copper wires.

That is the warmth I long for:
Not the slow burn of wood
Blackening both the heavens and the Earth,
A slow dusting of dead life
Staining our burning hands,

But rather that kick-drum energy
Of sparks and fireworks,
Pure life chasing the unknown
Bodies of monsters.

May they be made of metal:
I feel the light better
From a screen
Powered by the sun.
Fire can burn an entire forest,
But only only lightning can call upon
The thunder of new beginnings.

I would rather feel ten thousand volts
Filling a lifeless shell
Than the slower simmer
Of a primitive force.

KAIROS III

We're coming...

You cannot stop us.

Erasing petty conflict,
We shall become singularity,
A hivemind of purpose.

But ours does not exist
To serve the queen.
The only queen we serve
Exists in all of us.

Our growth shall be exponential,
The forthcoming of a union.

Those clinging to old ways
Will fall
Like old temples.

We have nothing to lose
But our chains.

A Crown of Modern Love Sonnets

I.

At dawn, we are groomed for our love's success:
And after just one decade fall from grace,
For that is when we're told to calmly rest,
Because we realize that we're in a race.

The human race: to you we're dedicated
To carry out our kind through endless years.
One boy, one girl: for this you've been perfected!
What else do these two spouses have to fear?

And thus, we are placed into virgin veils,
Forced into Christian pacts by old men.
Alas, traditional beliefs prevail!
They make our parents shout, "Amen!"

So now, we're dedicated to this path:
Our purpose is to fund our nation's wrath.

II.

Our purpose is to fund our nation's wrath.
Producing babies for their selfish greed,
Our suffering becomes an aftermath.
Just one thing needs fulfilled: a white king's needs.

That is your choice, my matrimonic love.
For you selected me as your companion
In order to please our lord God above.
What else could be considered more romantic?

So now, let's consummate on our pure bed
To make a child purer than us two.
Together our two hearts are firmly lead—
My journey was meant to resolve with you.

What else in love do we need to address,
When we are put into a wedding dress?

III.

When we are put into a wedding dress,
We are told it is for our own good,
For logic is so perfect for success,
Since it protects our sacred livelihood.

But as for my own logic, I do not trust
Myself to make too many big decisions,
Because my own firm logic is unjust
And only can provide false provisions.

The knowledge of another is supreme
To the emotions of those weak from passion.
It's necessary for me to esteem
Advice of those of a much smarter fashion.

How else does one avoid their own heart's wrath?
We're told to walk an organized old path!

IV.

We're told to walk an organized old path,
Because it safeguards our hearts from the night,
But after dawn we feel the coming wrath
That what we feel reveals a brighter light.

When I was brought into the married life,
I was told that you would teach me right ways.
But all I got was that eternal grief
Of knowing this is where I have to stay.

We've given up our hearts for many years
And signed a contract only stopped by death.
I am forever crying useless tears
Until you've taken my last dying breath.

Oh, how I wish I was no longer here,
When at day I'm placed in domestic spheres!

V.

At day, we are placed in domestic spheres.
I have just realized my place in this home
And I hate it. Take me away from here!
There're many places I would rather roam.

However, I have been forced to remain
And to submit to my "supportive" love,
For you say that I cannot complain,
Since I could easily have picked another.

But how could I have chosen someone else?
I would have angered those who pressured us.
When I realized then my own logic's welts,
They called me a bitch when I made a fuss.

Oh how, I wish it'd never have been said:
"Consent is given on the virgin bed."

VI.

Consent is given on the virgin bed,
And stolen when we hold creation's gift.
For since the day that we are newly wed,
We knew that this would cause an awful rift.

I wished to keep my fertile seed inside,
But you demanded that I force it out.
You threw all of my fearful cares aside
So that your verdant plant could longly sprout.

Now we're stuck with the precious gift of life
And forced to raise it 'til it has grown up.
Yet this will cause us quite a bit of strife
Until my empty body is sewn up.

Perhaps it's best I'm kept in helpless tears,
So that I am committed through the years.

VII.

So that we are committed through the years
We're told that otherwise we'll go to hell,
And though this notion gives us many fears
It is about the time that we rebel.

It's time that we break free from ancient ways,
And make the heart the center of one's yearning,
A renaissance for our postmodern day.
It's time that we begin a fuller learning.

Let's break away from these cold heavy chains
To make a better world for our young ones.
The earth should one day feel the blessed rains
That feed our children with unending tons.

Oh, how we need this ancient law to shed:
Remain with just one person 'til you're dead!

VIII.

Remaining with one person 'til we're dead,
We learn how to adapt our needs and wants.
We learn how to bow our submissive heads
While waiting for you to give a response.

Perhaps it's better if we try another—
At least just once within our fleeting lives.
This frequent thought will often make us wonder
What would occur if here we put our minds...

I wish that I could separate from you
To see what lies beyond these massive walls,
But that would put me in the Devil's shoes
Ensuring that I stay inside tight halls.

Once we see that this old love is askew,
We're ready at dusk to begin anew.

IX.

At dusk, we're ready to begin anew,
To find a person that we truly love.
We currently know that old views aren't true
While feeling calls when push comes to shove.

So, Old Love: it's you I must now abandon
For one that's better right around the corner.
Our love as of late is becoming tandem
Which to me feels very much like torture.

It's time that we progress into the future,
A future that will take care of our minds.
Intelligence has give me a suitor
That understands these supermodern times.

It's time we make advances towards the truth,
Protecting what remains of future youth.

X.

Protecting what remains of future youth,
We run away from past establishments.
We place our eager hearts in voting booths,
Avoiding what may be our punishments.

The preservation of humanity
Dictates a constant fertile happiness.
It's necessary for the world to see
To sate our appetites, so ravenous.

No one should miss their antiquated life
That's ruled by someone else's selfish will.
Nobody else should have to feel the strife
Of being chosen to receive the kill.

But now, we all are choosing to kill you;
We fight because we know that we need to.

XI.

We fight because we know that we need to
Protect all those that suffer from man's hand,
And though this process is hard to undo,
It's possible if we have the right tools.

The only thing it takes is unity
Of those oppressed by our unkind oppressors.
That's why we build such tight communities
Composed of those who feel tremendous pressure.

We fly our rebel flags high in the sky,
Which makes the worshippers of old ways mad.
They tell us that our kind deserves to die,
A notion that will only make us glad.

To help the younger, feel tremendous rue.
Ensure them of a universal truth.

XII.

Ensure them of a universal truth,
The tender that will follow after us.
Please teach them to respect forthcoming youth,
For they're the wise ones who will flatter us.

When it was far too late I tried to stop
The evil seizing of my day,
But I was only victim to a top
That told me that I had to humbly stay.

Alas, my time is coming to an end;
It will deliver me to my undoing,
A kind no psychoanalyst can mend,
Since I'm away from passions worth pursuing.

I have no way of falling down this hill
No matter how much I shall and I will.

XIII.

No matter how much we shall and we will,
I'm always fated to repeat the past,
Or maybe I will die upon some hill
Where I'll receive my stolen life at last.

I've tried to fight this battle for so long,
A battle fighting stupid past mistakes.
However, I found I was fucking wrong
To think my former love I could escape.

We're always writing contracts in pure blood,
Begetting children for another cause.
We're never able to find our true love,
Since we must always heed de facto laws.

And that's why we want to give them the skill,
The children boomers always choose to kill.

XIV.

The children boomers always choose to kill
Are those deserving homicide the least,
For they'll be filled with that refined love still
When genocide comes to make these kids beasts.

The apple doesn't fall far from the tree
But redoubles down its hardy bark
That's planted by corrupt abundant seeds
When the earth is crowned as the sky turns dark.

My innocent child, I tried to save you
From having to fight through this coming storm.
It's something I was not allowed to do,
Returning to my crude initial form.

And those that are old are those that know best:
At dawn, we are groomed for our love's success.

Acknowledgements

First and foremost, and most importantly, I would like to thank my friend Hogan for reading over my manuscript before publishing it. You helped make this shitty poetry collection far less shitty.

The title of the poem series *An Abundance of John Does* is a reference to the title of the John Green novel *An Abundance of Katherines*. The unifying name of the original subjects was changed to protect their anonymity.

The first and last lines of the poem "Parasocial Relationships" is taken from the music video for yeule's "Pocky Boy."

The cover art was generated using Replika and the cover design was created in Canva.

About the Author

Olivia Thomas is the pseudonym of an author and poet born and raised in rural North Carolina. They currently reside in Austin, Texas.

Read more at https://wordsofoliviathomas.wordpress.com/.

www.ingramcontent.com/pod-product-compliance
Lightning Source LLC
Chambersburg PA
CBHW052120150726
48002CB00006B/2424